OUTSIDE JOKES
Cartoons about nature and the outdoors

BETTY CHMIELNIAK GRACE

Second Edition
32 Additional Cartoons

Panther Creek Publishing
Albany, MO 64402
Copyright ©2005 by Betty C. Grace
ISBN 0-9725-3837-2
Cover Photo by Jim Grace
Printed by
Community Press, Inc.,
Chillicothe, MO 64601
(Thank you to Terry Schroll, Kim Ziegler
and the CP staff–BCG)

Printed on recycled paper

A Special Thank You
to the
Missouri Department of Conservation

For almost 20 years, I've had the small task
and big pleasure of drawing a monthly
cartoon for the
MISSOURI CONSERVATIONIST.
The cartoons in this collection first appeared
there. I appreciate the opportunity to reprint
them here.

To the many employees whose friendship
and encouragement I've enjoyed throughout
these years, I offer my sincere thanks.

To Ji

and

Jacob and Anna

"I'm sorry, but it does appear that we've lost it."

"And this is our den."

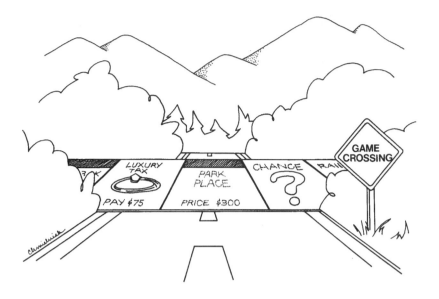

Origin of the term "toadstools"

SNAKE BIRD TURTLE

To the expert, turtle eggs
are easily recognized by their shells.

"Ptui! Nutrasweet!"

"You've changed..."

GARDEN FRESH
SALAD BAR

"You distract him and I'll go for the carrot."

"Do you have frogs' legs?"

"Picking fun, Gus?"

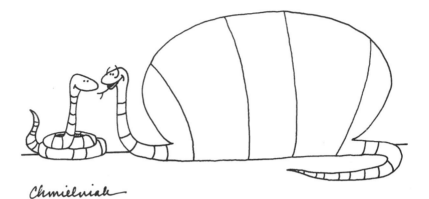

"On a summer day, *nothing* beats watermelon."

"I think he looks a little like both of us."

"Hibernate? I decided to *migrate* this year."

"But archery season is closed."

Mushroom hunting strategy

"The pickings sure have improved since
we took down the deer crossing sign."

"Go ahead, but remember what happens
to the early worm."

"Thanksgiving!?! Bah, humbug!"

"I need permits to keep seven swans-a-swimming,
six geese-a-laying, four calling birds, three French hens,
two turtle doves and a partridge-in-a-pear-tree."

"So what if we look cool–unless we quit using
this styling mousse, we'll never get our
feathers back down."

Bass–bass   Grouse–drums   Swan–trumpeter

"Ah, forget her. There are plenty of other fish in the sea."

"Hum, hum hum! Why don't you guys ever learn some words?"

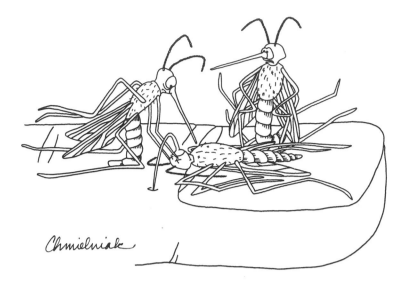

"Estelle never could stand the sight of blood."

"Line's busy, fly again."

"If you ask me, it's a trap."

"You can always pick out the migrants."

An insomniac hibernator

"Hello, Room Service? I'd like a wake-up call for February 2nd."

"So the fish were biting, eh?"

"Sometimes he just likes to sit
in a small tree and pretend he's a big bird."

"I don't think this liquid diet is
keeping your weight off, Lorraine."

"Darn this farmer's tan!"

"Tell me, what does someone so
cultivated see in someone so wild?"

28

"I hope you've washed up for dinner."

"Sorry boys, the limit's two."

Multiplying like rabbits

February 14th

Chmielniak

"I hate these processed foods."

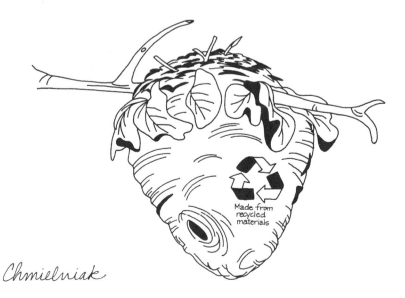

Made from
recycled
materials

Chmielniak

"Mrs. Howard? Daryl won't be in
school today–he's got a frog in his throat."

"See you ate 'er, alligator."

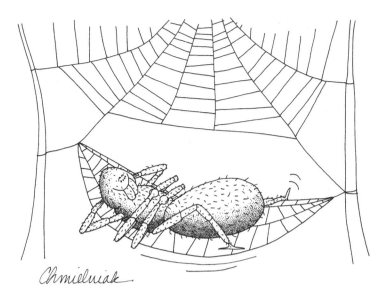

"Heads he's yours, tails he's mine."

"Hey waiter, there's no fly in my soup."

"Hey Tom, I almost didn't recognize you with a beard!"

Mistletoads

"Agh! Everything I eat goes right to my hips."

"I've had it with your obsession to be
the first robins back each spring."

"I hate velcro."

"Hey, over there...those two look like a couple of fish out of water."

"When you asked me to a picnic for a bite to eat, this wasn't what I had in mind."

"That's what I want to be when I grow up."

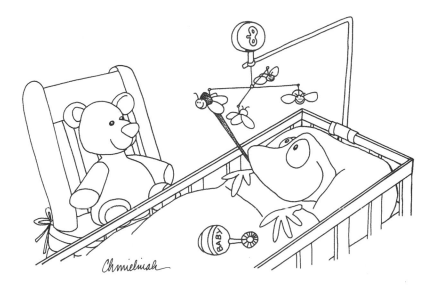

"There are largemouth bass and smallmouth bass,
and then there's Mildred—the bigmouth bass."

"Bob says if he's got to fall,
he's wearing a bungie cord."

"Geez, my stomach's in knots over this."

It was spring. Frogs were calling everywhere.

"Looks like housing starts are up this month."

"To them it's garbage. To me it's junk food."

"Boy those things give me the creeps."

Frog days of summer

"I'm flattered by your interest, Richard, but I wish I could be sure you were attracted to my mind and not just my pheromones."

"Mom, Daryl's being gross. He says he's eating spaghetti."

"The birds with the white heads and tails are mature eagles and the ones with dark heads and tails are amateur eagles."

"I know it's the night before Christmas, but with last minute cards to write, presents to wrap and the tree still to decorate, it's hard not to stir."

"Cold enough for you?"

Why a crayfish kid hates to have its great aunt visit

Why opossums are not popular playmates

"The more of this I see, the more
I'm beginning to think there's no intelligent life out there."

"On a day like this, I just gotta get out and stretch my legs."

When ant picnics are invaded by humans

Survival of the fittest

"Lyle, quit reading the 'Nutrition Facts.'
You're getting on my nerves."

"Have a safe trip. Call us when you get there."

"If you ask me, Rudolph is getting to be a regular old windbag."

"He hasn't moved in days. I say we eat him."

February 2nd

"Hey guys, listen. The woodpecker's into rap!"

Mushroom hunting bag limit: Two

"There's one that looks like a dragon. And that one's a castle. And right overhead... it looks like a hawk diving..."

DEAR, WAKE UP. YOU'RE BLINKING IN YOUR SLEEP AGAIN.

"There goes Wanda with her new boyfriend.
Now what rock do you suppose she found him under?"

"You just can't beat food right off the grille."

"Hey Vic, we're *herbivores*. According to this guy's driver's license, we just ate Herb."

Some scientists believe certain birds migrate at night and somehow use star patterns to find direction.

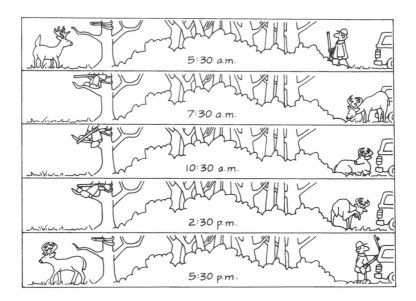

Opening Day

One froggy Christmas Eve

"Why do we even bother taking pictures when everyone's always got the same dumb expression?"

Under certain circumstances, a bird band
can adversely effect the bird's ability to fly.

A scene from Mockingbird family life

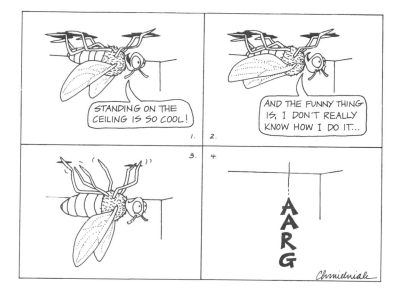

"He hasn't been out since the thing's been installed."

Understandably, parents worried about the new
crossing guard's qualifications.

In their spare time, baby boomer entomologists
like to reminisce about their favorite beetle.

"You won. The tortoise tested positive for steroids."

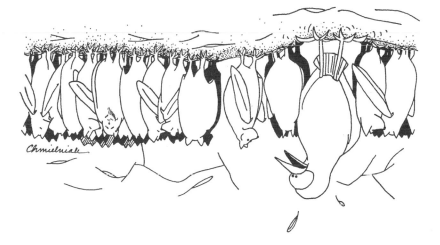

"I never should have let you talk me into this."

"Trust me, Irene. Here's a place you're sure to meet a guy."

"I wonder how jolly the old boy will be
when he sees we've pitched his sack of toys."

"I keep having this horrible dream where I fall into
a deep pit and it's full of people with hoes."

"Why is it, Howard, that whenever you're feeling romantic,
you have to start that incessant calling?"

"Oh great. It looks like the Orioles are back and headed this way with their migration videos"

"After his time in the military and all those years with the post office, getta load of that pension check."

"I've zinged folks on doorknobs and handrails, but nothing's more fun than just hovering around them when they're behind the wheel."

"Excuse me, but the Mrs. and I wondered if you could keep an eye on the youngsters while she and I step out for just a bit."

A ranger once suggested to Warren that he "Take only pictures, leave only footprints." Muddled by the advice, Warren now takes only pictures of footprints.

During the astral observatory's off hours, Professor Keller liked to fix the great telescope on remote corners of the earth and do a little birdwatching.

"Hey buddy, why the long face?"

"Remember when we thought that the best thing
about the suburbs was raiding the garbage?"

"I've never seen a bird like that before—must
be some weird winter migrant."

"It must have been a cold night. I see the pikes are frozen."

Groundhog Day, 5:00 a.m.

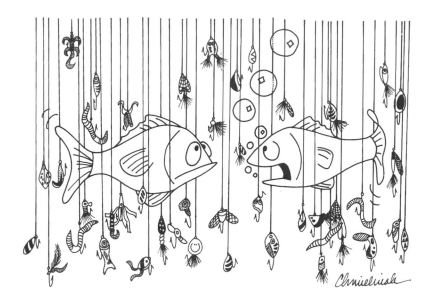

"Must be Opening Day."

"Old Hansen next door will be hard
pressed to find one bigger than this baby."

"Delores, whatever happened to instinct?!"

"You know Larry, we've been married so long that I think
we're beginning to look alike."

"She told her friend, 'If you don't bother them, they won't bother you,' and I just had to prove her wrong!"

How we hear birds   How birds hear each other

"Go ahead and fly. When I travel, I like
to see the sights along the way."

77

"Time to count our blessings, Ike. It's the day
after Thanksgiving and you and I are leftovers."

"Don't act suspicious. If mom finds out we ate
the candy canes, we'll be in big trouble."

"Now make a wish and then huff and puff
and blow your candles out."

"Well Bentley, so much for all that
'no two exactly alike' business."

"There just don't seem to be any *really* big ones this year."

"I hate heavy rains. They always make the worms soggy."

"Go fish."

"All that time I worked for the big colony,
I always dreamed of retiring to a little farm like this."

"I can take this humidity, but I can't stand the heat."

"You kids look both ways before crossing the creek.
I don't want you getting hit by a gar."

"Well Alice, it looks like my Victor has a non-typical rack this year, but I think he'll be pretty handy around the house."

"The only thing more satisfying than a window feeder is the window feeder at a house with an indoor cat."

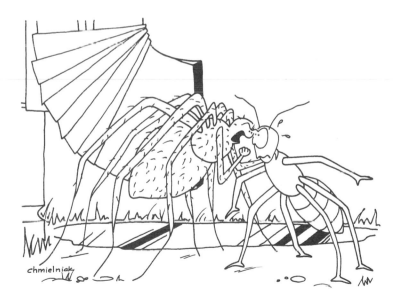

"Hey buddy, around here it's 'itsy bitsy' not 'eency weency.'"

"Hey, they oughtta be recycling this stuff!"

86

"How can you kids be such picky eaters?
You're *maggots*, for goodness sake."

"If we play hooky, just what are we gonna' do?"

"Good news, mole. You're not blind, you just have tunnel vision."

"I hate August. There's always tar on my feet and tar in my food."

The night before migration starts

"Lyle, quit humming 'King of the Road,' and just go."

"That may be fun Eddie, but those are lousy snow angels."

February 2nd, 5:00 a.m.: A groundhog flips on the bedroom light and inadvertently dooms everyone to six more weeks of winter.

Hansel and Gretl as adults

"...and so the beautiful frog kissed the ugly prince. All at once,
he turned into a handsome frog. They were soon married and
lived happily ever after."

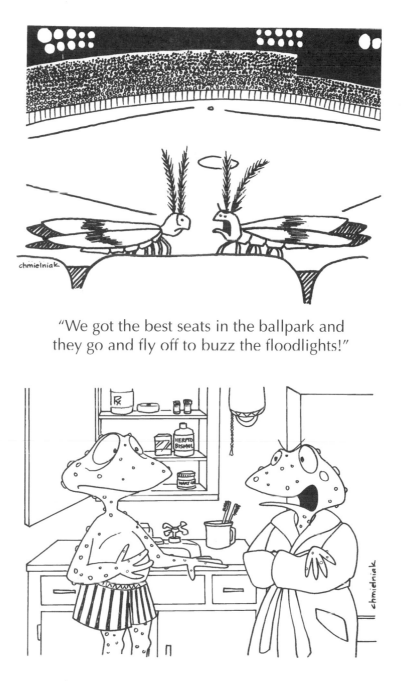

"We got the best seats in the ballpark and they go and fly off to buzz the floodlights!"

"Heartburn?!? Have you been eating fireflies again?"

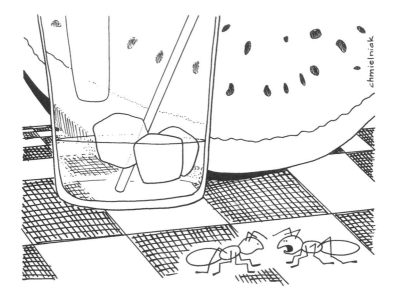

"Everything looks great but stay away from the deviled eggs and potato salad. They've been out in the sun all day."

When there's no one around and the fence looks too high

What the late bird gets

"Rats! We play the herons in the first game."

"... and so the waiter asks me, 'Would you like a table for you and the ladybug?' And I say to him, 'Hey buddy, that's no ladybug, that's my wife!'"

When insects become stand-up comedians

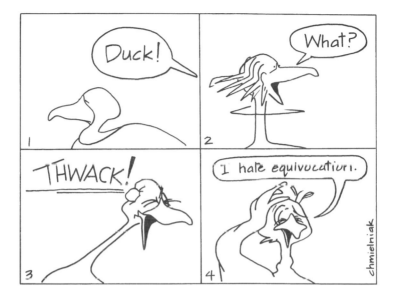

"First, we were tadpoles. Now we're frogs. I wonder what's next?"

"What a stomachache! I must
have eaten something that wasn't spoiled."

"This is exactly how I pictured it!"

"He's been like this ever since they started minting those special state quarters."

"He's completely run down. Better go get some jumper cables."

"Phew! Just our luck to get seated next to
a buzzard with carrion luggage."

"I can never remember,
are we reptiles or amphibians?"

"At first, it bothered me.
Now it's got me thinking about getting a tattoo."

Ill-adapted for midnight snacking,
Bob freezes in the refrigerator light.

"Fruitcake—my favorite holiday tradition."

"Well for heaven's sake, Gloria. Didn't you know you're supposed to drain that thing in the fall?"

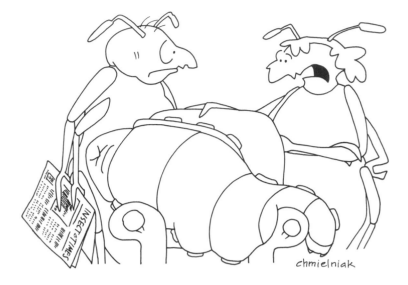

"I just can't believe our dear, sweet, lovable larva
has developed into this sullen, sleepy, obnoxious pupa!"

"They *never* buy anything–they're browsers."

"Before you go, we need to arrange to review the proofs, at which time we'll negotiate model fees and discuss printing rights."

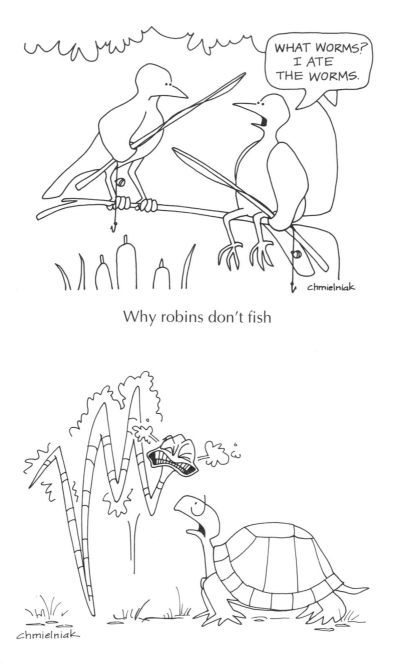

Why robins don't fish

"Never thought much about it Pete, but I guess poison ivy and insect bites would be a real problem for you."

chmielniak

"This time she just stood her ground
and creamed me with the curds and whey."

chmielniak

Geese migrating in vees

Geese migrating in Humvees

"Here's a weird coincidence. Only the adult males
have beards. The females and immatures don't."

The rabbit family has its picture taken.

"Forget 'metamorphosis.'
I prefer to think of it as 'an extreme makeover.'"

"The wife and I decided not to built this year.
We found ourselves this nice little fixer-upper instead."

"They don't build much of a nest
but they sure lay a lot of eggs."

"It's a treat to come back to a home-cooked meal
after eating all week on the road."

"You're lucky to be the oldest–when you're
the 1,613th, you're always overlooked."

As development encroaches on wildlife habitat,
it's common to see deer moving into suburban neighborhoods.

The day before Opening Day   Opening Day

"Hey Santa, the flying squirrels convinced
the reindeer to let them pull the sleigh."

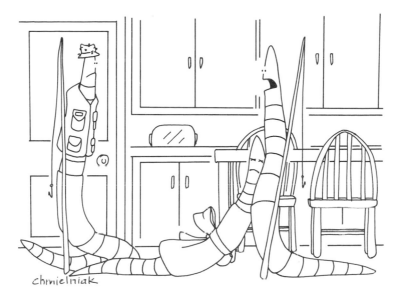

"I told her you and I were going fishing, and she fainted."

"If you ask me, she's a regular control freak."

"Hey guys, we *fly on* thermals, we don't *wear* them."

"No, your class will *not* watch him turn into a frog.
Now take your baby brother out of that jar
and put him back where he belongs."